LOVE and other expressions of the SELF

Jane Ellen Newell, Ph.D.

innovativeink PUBLISHING
A Division of Kendall Hunt

www.innovativeinkpublishing.com
Send all inquiries to:
4050 Westmark Drive
Dubuque, IA 52004-1840

Print ISBN: 979-8-3851-3020-7
Ebook ISBN: 979-8-3851-3021-4

Published in the United States of America

DEDICATION

For Gautama,
In whom, being my mirror,
I saw
My True Self

CONTENTS

INTRODUCTION

In my experience, the return to God, the return to Love, and the return to Self are all interchangeable and interrelated. A shift or change in one area impacts all. And when, in the living of life, awareness arises of these three as One, it is time to give Voice to the experience.

This little book of poems is just that: My experience finding its Voice. May you find in these pages, identification, if you will – or alignment, discovery, or even questioning and doubt.

May your reading give rise to your experience and your Voice.

Dr. Jane Newell

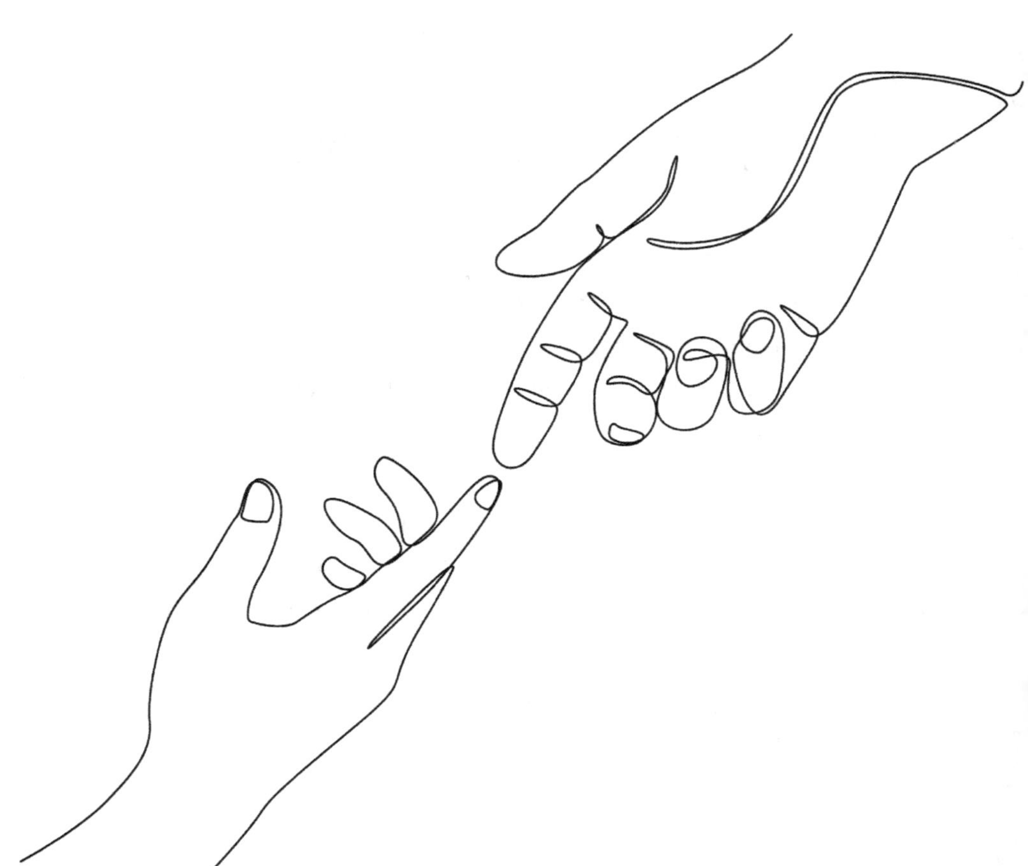

CHAPTER 1

First Expressions

God, I believe.

But what

Why

How?

So many questions

I would long to have answered.

Jane Ellen Scott

Age 12

Published in School Newspaper

CHAPTER 2
Abandoned To Love

Abandon

Love...what have you
Done to me?
I foolishly
Called out Your name.

No reasoning
Can save me now
Lost in a feeling
Of forever

No edge
To where you started
You have always
Been with me

One moment, one breath
And there You were
New, but as ancient
As before all time

Now and then
and yet to come...
Love

CHAPTER 3
Identity

Who Am I Now?

Who am I?

I ask for the

Millionth time

While on the journey

Through this life

Of mine.

Who am I now? I ask,

A new question.

A new "who" from a new place

A new "Love" from a new grace.

Who am I now?

CHAPTER 4
Discovery

The Mystery of Love

You, the very thing I long for
You, the very Mystery unknown
You, I will follow
For I have no other choice

What your face looks like
How your voice might sound
What your workings may be
Are all a Mystery to me

Love...
You have found me
My soul has opened wide
You are all I long for
I see You everywhere

I hear You in the birdie
Chirping sweet nothings to me
My heart stirs, my soul opens
It's You singing to me
And I, I sing to You too

Love...
I see You in the roses
Rising so gently
From the earth
Your beauty takes me over
Love has found me

I feel You in the touch
Of hand to hand
And heart to heart
Your mystery yet to unfold

Felt deep within
A place of no end
Eye to eye and soul to soul
Love engulfs without warning

I taste You in the cherry's
Piqued flavor
Designed to arouse my soul
I smell You in the fragrance
Of the roses, and lilacs...
And baked bread

Love...
You occupy me
I have no space but Your Presence
Nowhere for me to go
Nor would I want to now
For You have saved me

I plunge full-headed
Full-hearted
Over the edge I go
You have found me
And I have found You too

Everywhere I go
All that I see
All I taste
The sounds,
The feels,
The smells...
All are You.

Love...
You have captured me
Where shall we go?

Plaything

Love...

You tease me

You stir me to my soul

You draw me

Nowhere I'd rather be

Love...

You have slain me

And risen me as well

There is no place

That You are not

Love...

I seek to know You

To understand You – my way

But You, you'll have none of it

The Mystery You remain

Surrender to the Mystery

Surrender, then I will

Surrender, then I have

No form will You take

To make it easy on me

Won't You kindly

Conform to my will?

Won't You put Yourself

In neat little boxes

With labels on for me

To know when You're there

Or where You're not

Oh…how silly of me,

A fool's folly

To try to contain

The Source of it all

Surrender, then I must

Surrender, then I do

Surrender to the Love that owns me.

I surrender, Love, to You.

CHAPTER 5
Embodied

Dancing

Dancing between
The realms
Of light and love
I found you.

This mystery of life
Of crash
And burn
And rise from the ashes...
Love.

How can it be
That once we were
And now we are
But soon we shall be
No more?

This "you"
And this "me"
And for a time,
There was this "we."

In His garden
Pray we did
And pray we do
And love, sweet love
I felt for you.

How cruel this human realm
Can be
To feel the tender
Opening to love
And...the closing of the door.

Would I now regret
The opening,
Though now it's filled
With tears?

Never, never, never
Not in a million years.
For that is likely
How long I've loved you
And another million
To go

Love has captured me

Love will not let me go

But you, my darling,

You, I will surrender.

Surrender you to

Love.

The love that has

No beginning and

Without question

No end

The love that will

Hold you tenderly

Even when I cannot.

Loving You

Loving you was not
My choice
This, I hope you understand.
There was darkness
And pain and sorrow
And dread...
Then, there was you.
And in the light
You opened for me
A path unfolded
To the Divine.
A flight to the heavens
A drop into the soul
And there you were
As though
You'd always been.
And now
You shall always be
A part
In the heart
Of me.

Goodbye

Goodbye is something
I cannot say
It suggests
We'll go away.

How can there be
An end
To what has no beginning
But has always been?

They say lovers don't find
One another,
They discover that they've
Always been within.

A lover of my soul
You've been
If not my body, true
And I, your lover too.

For your soul
Is as light to me
Illuminating my darkness

With you
I came to Being
Alive in both body
And soul.

Goodbye I cannot say
For in my heart
You will always stay.

How bitter is this
Pill I swallow
Loving you and
Letting go.

Letting go to what?
I have no clue.
But loving you?
For me there is no end.

No goodbyes
For in my heart
You will always be.

Need

You ask me what I
Need.
My wobbly heart,
Like a newborn lamb,
Hesitates.
"I don't know," I say.

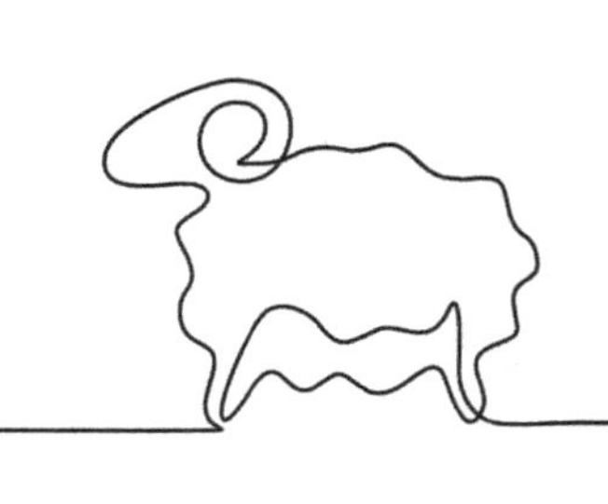

But I do know.
It's simply that this
Part of me
Has had no voice
For so long

That forming the words
Is like
Learning to walk,
From nothing.
Hard stop.
No movement.
No muscle on the bone.
Herculean strength.

And so, it is

With a heart

Cut off from

Its blood supply,

Love.

When love came online,

Flowing

Into these once

Blocked arteries,

It felt good,

Really, really good.

But it was foreign

To this heart

Of mine.

What is this strange

Elixir?

What planet have I

Landed on?

What chemicals
Have jump-started
This frozen heart?
And where did *you* come from?

Like an

Oxygen-starved

Brain,

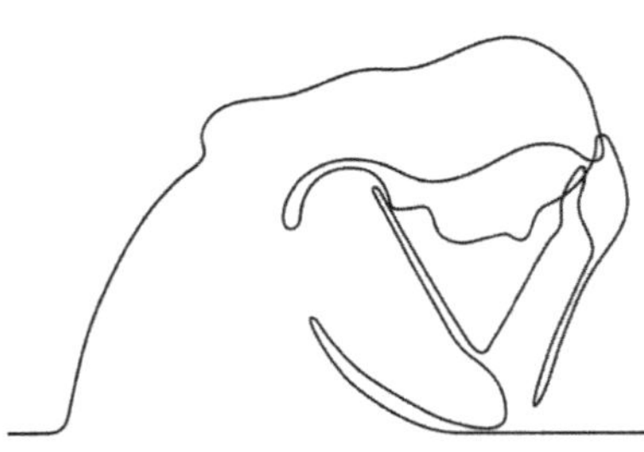

My mind could not

Make sense.

And with no words
For description,
My voice remained
Inaudible
Like the sound of
One hand clapping

All feeling, no sound emerging
Only the gushing
Of a newly-beating-heart
Pumping now,
With this new life-force:
Love.

Need was not

Something

This heart understood.

Having suffered

Ischemia of the heart,

The lack of love.

As debilitating

As no oxygen to the brain

This heart dared not

To say

"I need you"

It could not find

Its way

To risk such

Life-threatening

Nakedness.

But that was then,

And this is now.

Today, a new day,

And I a new Self.

The heart pumping
Fully now
Filled with radiant
Love.

The New Self knows
Who she is.
And what she needs.

Her wobbly legs
Now firm.
Her once silent voice
Now sighing and singing
And shouting
With the Joy of life.

Her body, now alive
Infused with
Eternal light and Love,
The Love that has no beginning
And no end.

Embodied now, she feels.

And knows her needs.

And her voice

Serves her well.

Out from the depths

Of the heart

Her truth emerges...

Union.

Of both body and soul

With another

Embodied one.

Alive, embodied,

Feeling, needing,

Knowing now.

Love has found me.

I am Alive.

I Love You. I Hate You

To the one

With whom love came through,

The one with whom

This heart

Woke from its sleeping.

Not sleeping

Like a tender nap

On a Sunday afternoon.

No, sleeping like unto death.

The kind of sleeping

Where one

Can not hear, or see, or taste,

Smell or touch what love is

For the danger of it

Is so real.

And then there was you.

No words did you speak

That would

This death undo.

No, no, not in speaking
Did life and love
come through.

From death to life,
To love broken through,
In your presence

The nothingness of silence
And you...
Love broke through

A heavy burden
To bare
For a mere man, it's true.

Yet, it was Love Itself
That found me.
A pure Traveler in you.

You, the vehicle,
Its Presence to deliver –
A gift flown in

From the Divine
To me, for me, through you.

Thank you,
Though you could not stay.
And I love you.
And I hate you.
And I miss you, it's true.

And there's nothing,
Nothing, nothing...
Nothing to do.
Only to give Voice
To the feeling of you.

Musing and Missing

Musing now of passions missed

By not hearing

What was unspokenly said

Through tender eyes,

A slight tilt of the head, or

Straight-on-eye-contact,

Light smile behind

Stone exterior

Who were you?

I wish I had known

How To ask,

To discover you

And...a new me.

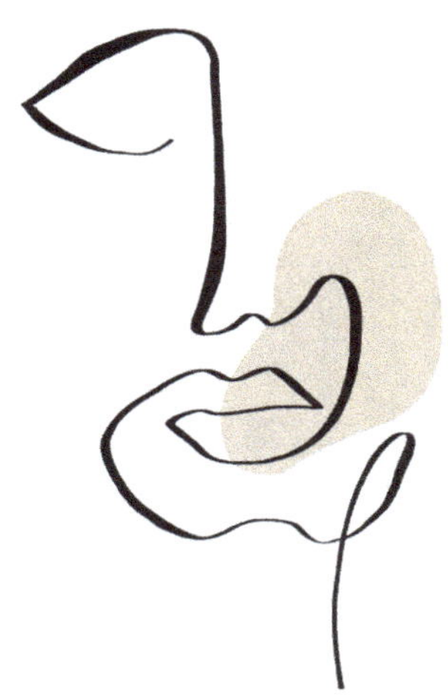

The Keys

A voice unexpectedly rang out

"….so-and-so would dance with you

In the Unknown" I think I heard.

But for the dozen

Other souls gathered

And the words flowing,

I could not fully hear,

Or…take it in.

And succumbing to a kind of pride

Wrapped in disbelief,

I said nothing,

Nodding a nod of acknowledgement.

Acknowledging what?

What great adventure

Did I say "yes" to

But failed to pick up the keys?

Which keys may have opened

The door to

A room that is warm

And friendly, or

Wildly on fire with love.

Or yet another door,

To a car

Meandering down a forlorn

Hidden dusty road

Upon which,

If I had ridden,

We may have taken that branch

Of the path

That led to

The highway

Where we zoomed,

Lightspeed into the unknown,

Yet-to-be-discovered land

Of the fleshy-flying-wispy

Selves we are.

And I find myself weeping

For what might have been.

My Body My Teacher

Body, my body – Teacher of mine,

Forgive me, for deaf I have been.

No sound of the whispers

Of love, did I hear

If ever they were

Whispered to me.

Such blindness

Did keep me from seeing

Soft and strong beauty

When danced it did

Before my view,

Blocked by

The terror of seeing beauty

For what it is.

How is it that

The fragrance of love

Had been perceived

As danger

In its expression?

Lost, but more truly-stated,

Never found.

A lifetime of passion

Not once perceived

For what it was,

Or could have been

An invitation to life

To living

To unfolding,

A molding of the Self

How tragically bland,

My tastebuds

For love had been.

Never fully evolved

Stopped before

They had the chance

At life,

At love,

Or tasting the sweetness...

Aye – missed was the fullness

Of savoring, that can be known

By the one who

Will bite deep and full

And surrender

To its flavors unfolding

On the vine

Perceived by this taster of mine

Bitter tears

Now fall, seeing and hearing,

Smelling and tasting too…

All to full-body, the feeling of you.

Which feeling

Gives rise to its breaking of the dam

Alive, alive

Body, my body – Dear Teacher of Mine

CHAPTER 6
Survivor

SURVIVOR

Survivor – I AM

How strong and courageous

To say so, it's true.

Once trapped in a lifetime of silence,

My Voice now freed

Does sing...

I AM ALIVE HERE...

Hear me, I pray.

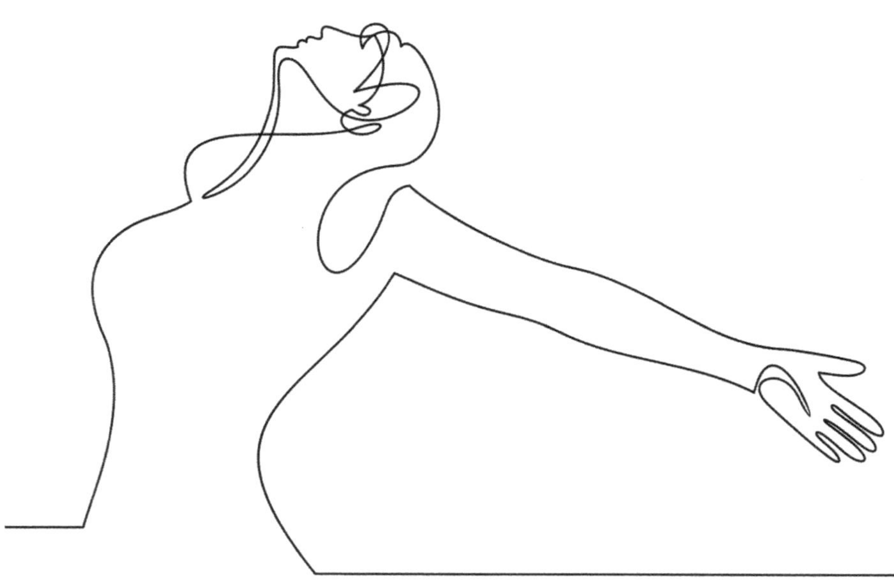

CHAPTER 7
New Identity

Walking Me

How to express

The gratitude

I have for you

Is not possible in

These few words

But gratitude I have

And love

That expands over eons

You, my dear friend,

Have been

Walking me

Back

To

My Self.

I have arrived.

Love, Jane

New Identity Declaration

1. I am a Child of God.
   As His Child,
   I am worthy of all
   Creation

2. Because I am his Child
   He loves me

3. The Love I long for in other humans
   Is the longing
   I have for God Himself –
   And His Love

4. As a living Child of God
   Love is my birthright
   I am never without the love of God.

5. The messages and experiences
   Of this world are a part of Maya,
   The cosmic delusion.

6. I am free from the domination
   Of Maya
   Because I know who I Am.

7. I am so deeply loved by God
   That he is playing
   Hide-and-seek with me.

8. I am experiencing the
Love of the Divine
Breaking into my world.

9. I live in my body.
Yogananda called it
My "garment"

10. I love my body.
It is beautiful.
I will care for my body
With love and appreciation.

11. While I seek God first
Above all things
And all people
Still, I am blessed to love
And be loved by others
While I am in this body.

12. My body brings pleasure
To me
As I wear it like a garment
I love the feeling of being adorned
In this body
I am fearfully and wonderfully made.

13. In the same way
That I love to adorn my body
With beautiful clothing – full of color
And design, and playfulness –
So also, my soul loves
To be adorned with my body.

14. I imagine my soul
Looking out at
The Garment
She is wearing.
She loves to feel good
In her Garment.

15. My body
Is the way
My Soul experiences
This realm of life.

16. My soul wants to feel life:
To laugh, play, love
To sing, dance, make love
To weep and shout,
To touch and be touched
To see and be seen
To taste and smell,
To hear and be heard
To create and destroy
To inhale and exhale
To run, walk, dream, smile, cry
To embrace and be embraced

17. I am passion.
I am the passion
Of creation itself.
The explosion of life
Is who I am.
Feeling passion is feeling life.

18. I am love.
Love is expressed through me.
Those I love
Are loved by Love itself.

19. I am Light.
I am the light of God.
The light, which is God,
Expresses itself through me,
As me, for me,
And for others.

20. I am Creation.
The creative mind of God
Dwells in me,
Seeking expression in the world
Through me.

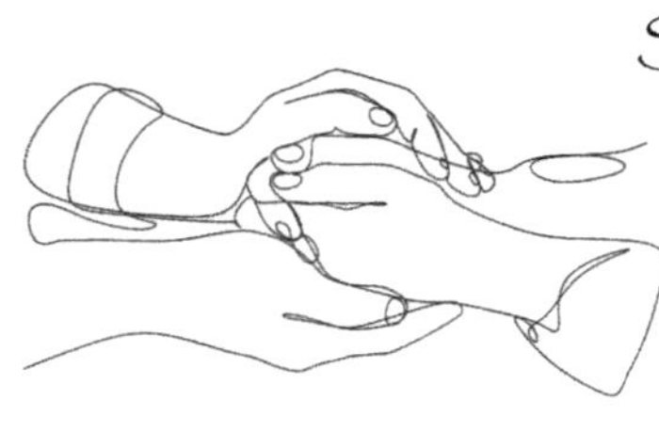

21. I am Service.
I express my love for God
By serving others.
Serving others
Is serving God in each one
And the world.

22. I am the Sound of God.
My voice is the
Voice of God.
Every word, every song,
Every moan and sigh, all sound
Is the expression of God, The
Breath of God.

23. I am the Beloved of God.
God seeks me out
And I seek God too,
We love one another.

24. I am a Treasure of God.
Priceless and honored.
And treated with the tenderness
Of care that cherishes
All the parts of me.

25. I am the Beauty of God.
God gazes upon me
And weeps
For the joy of experiencing
My beauty, the beauty that is God.

26. I am the Mind of God.
Thinking, wondering,
Pondering and contemplating.
God contributes to humanity
Through me.

I am the Pearl of Great Price.
Whose value has no figure,
For
I
was
Formed
In
The
Turmoil
Of
The
Shell
Of
Life
Itself
I AM Jane.
Yahweh is merciful
Let it be so.

EPILOGUE

I was born into a complex family system. We all experienced a
great deal of trauma due to incestual sexual abuse and alco-
holism in our family. Incest is a difficult trauma to name and heal
from – because, 1) as children we have no idea of what is hap-
pening, 2) it impacts developmental processes on many levels,
most importantly, the sense of self, 3) it affects all relationships,
especially romantic, intimate ones, and 4) it is shrouded in secre-
cy, which of course, keeps it in place. While it is experienced as
an individual occurrence, it is much, much more than that – it is a
global, societal pandemic. Most estimates indicate that one in
four women will experience sexual abuse sometime in their lives.
Incest, due to its hidden nature, is not as well documented, but
some estimates are as high as 15 % – 18% of people worldwide,
have experienced or are now experiencing incest.

While my early childhood trauma affected all areas of my life, I
am blessed to have a huge family – all of whom I love and adore
– and they me. My eldest of three daughters, was born to me
when I was 16 years of age. Each have gone on to create their
own lives and beautiful families. My daughters were all affected

by my trauma – each in different ways. And, as incest is a family infiltrator, impacting everyone for generations to come, we are all healing in our own ways over time. It is my prayer that as I have found my voice, they each will find and use theirs.

I have spent my entire adult life seeking to understand my early family life, to heal, to transform my life, and to make a contribution to humanity. That is the purpose of sharing my poetry now – as a contribution to individuals and families who have or are experiencing incestual sexual abuse – and anyone who is experiencing now or in the past, abuse of any kind. As we have come to understand, that is nearly all of us, on some level. You may relate to my expressions of Self. I share my writing with the world, in order to give Voice to the unspeakable. May it be a blessing.

I started my career of service to humanity as a social worker and parent educator. Working in the prevention of child abuse, I imagined that working with parents would be the most effective way of serving children – by providing education and support to struggling families. After working in the field of adoption, specifically, youth aging-out-of-foster care, I wondered, "What is family?" and I returned to graduate school, earning my master's and doctorate degrees in family social science.

As fate would have it, I was assigned in my doctoral teaching practicum to teach intimate relationship development and – my inner world collided with my outer professional development world – and my dissertation was born. Inspired by reading the autobiographical stories of intimate relationship development for hundreds of college students, and always informed by my own experience of isolation and lack of intimacy, my 4-dimensional model was born.

As a child who survived familial sexual trauma, I separated from myself to survive, and had no sense of being worthy of love. Love has always been the mystery for me, the unreachable star – as in the Man of La Mancha. Healing from the trauma was, as one of my earliest therapists said to me, "like pealing back the layers of an onion." I can still remember the feeling in my gut and my first instinctive thought when I heard this, "Oh shit, I'm going to be here a long, long time." More than 30 years later and I'm still pealing back the layers.

What I've discovered is that God, Love, and Self all flow together in an iterative, interrelated, and transformative process. Any movement in one area impacts a breakthrough in all: It's holistic. Ultimately, I have experienced Divine Love as the underpinning, overarching, and pervasive essence throughout my journey of being alive. This process has taken me back to the beginning – and through healing and transformation – to the present. I have returned to the original intended state of Being: One with God, Love, and my Self.

My deepest love and appreciation go to my 92-year-old mother, Betty, who saved us by divorcing our father and starting a new life in the 1960s, when being a woman was challenging enough, much less to be a single mother of three. She did it! Thanks, Mom. She gave me her blessing to tell my (our) story, as well as my sister, Susan, a retired medical doctor and lawyer, who herself is a survivor. As a ground-breaking pediatric neonatologist and endocrinologist, you inspired me as I pursued my Ph.D. later in life. My brother Stephen, who died by suicide – and who is still very much present with me – I love you. For my three daughters: Jessica, Rachel, and Eliza – who gave me my reason for living – I love you each deeply and eternally. To my grandchildren, who bring me such joy, my niece, nephew and friends, thank you, I adore you all. Gratitude and love to my brother-of-choice, Tom, with whom I continue to know the love of a brother. Deepest love and appreciation of my soul sister, Elizabeth, for the joy and support of our friendship on this journey. New worlds of possibility opened to me through my participation with Landmark Worldwide, and I'm so grateful. My doctoral advisors and mentors Paul, Tai, Cathy & Cynthia – without whom, I would not have emerged as Dr. Newell, I love and respect each of you. To healers of all sorts, I thank you, and in particular, Gautama, to whom this book is dedicated. In his non-judgmental, profound offering of sacred love, he became my mirror by which I was able to see my true Self.

In love & service,

Dr. Jane Newell

CONTACT INFO

"If life is the story of love we live, be the hero of your own story."

Dr. Jane Newell

Love's Hero, LLC

Dr. Jane Newell

drjane@loveshero.com

and janenewell8899@gmail.com

Love's Hero, LLC provides seminars, coaching, and consultation. Dr. Newell is available for speaking engagements. Contact Dr. Jane for a complementary consultation to discover the many ways you may benefit from Love's Hero's offerings.

www.ingramcontent.com/pod-product-compliance
Lightning Source LLC
Chambersburg PA
CBHW070322160726
47999CB00003B/1107